A SUMMARY, REVIEW &
ANALYSIS OF

DAN HARRIS'

10% HAPPIER

HOW I TAMED THE VOICE IN
MY HEAD

BY

SAVE TIME SUMMARIES

Note to Readers: We encourage you to first order a copy of Dan Harris' full book, _10% Happier: How I Tamed the Voice in My Head, Reduced Stress Without Losing My Edge, and Found Self-Help That Actually Works--A True Story_ before you read this unofficial Book Summary & Review. Most readers use this guide by first reading a chapter from the full copy, and then reading the corresponding section from this Book Summary & Review. Others prefer to read the entire book from cover-to-cover, and then review using this review and analysis.

Other Amazon Kindle Ebooks from *Save Time Summaries:*

Summary of Dr. Mark Hayman's *The Blood Sugar Solution 10-Day Detox Diet: Activate Your Body's Natural Ability to Burn Fat and Lose Weight Fast*

Summary of Dr. David Permutter's *Grain Brain: The Surprising Truth about Wheat, Carbs, and Sugar*

Summary of Robert Lustig's *Fat Chance - - Battling Sugar, Obesity & Disease*

Summary of Stephen Covey's *The 7 Habits of Highly Effective People*

TABLE OF CONTENTS

OVERVIEW

We all have a little voice in our head that encourages us to raid the cookie jar after a day of healthy eating. Sometimes, thankfully, it pushes us to try harder. This inner voice can provide a positive impact on your life, but it can sometimes create an overwhelming noise in your head that simply creates anxiety, stress, and worry. Dan Harris' *10% Happier* chronicles the journey of Dan Harris in trying to find a way to tame his inner voice and achieve greater balance in his life.

While Harris is a more public figure than most readers, his commentary provides reassurance that his inner voice is just as vocal as that of anyone. The inner voice that drove him to be career-oriented and strive to be at the top of his field also provided a constant stream of worry and self-criticism. This harsh and critical form of inner voice can be responsible for addictions, esteem issues, and severe self-doubt. This makes it a relevant issue for those whose little voice has told them not to go for a promotion or put themselves out there, as they would only fail.

Harris' *10% Happier* follows the career and inner commentary of Dan Harris, from his early journalist days through career crisis and self-doubt, on to a sense of calm and achievement. While many people are skeptical of meditation, Harris takes a realistic view and asks the questions many people are keen to ask but lack the opportunity or bravery to do so.

The book is a great read for anyone who is struggling to manage inner voices. If you have found yourself repeatedly churning over what to say or do before taking any action, *10% Happier* could be the key to improving your happiness. The book is completely relevant to today's audience, as most people are struggling to maintain the balance between the cutthroat demands of the modern business world while retaining a sense of being calm. Harris details the competitive edge needed in the world of television news and journalism. He explains the constant need to be on the air and pushing forward, which people from all industries may appreciate. This need for constant innovation and performance has left many people feeling doubt about their own abilities and envious of their colleagues. However, through Harris' journey, it is easy to see that they are not alone.

Harris' *10% Happier* explores the concept of living in the moment, as well as the importance of meditation. While many people have a biased view of meditation, it is becoming a mainstream approach to reducing stress and improving mental well-being. Many dedicated followers of Buddhism may dislike the capitalist view of using the fundamentals of Buddhism to succeed in the workplace. However, Harris does explore many of the religious aspects to finding a quieter inner voice. This journey from stressed news journalist to a man who is "10% happier" will appeal to those on the road to personal development, whether they have tried meditation before or are new to the concept.

PREFACE

SUMMARY

The preface covers the internal monologue, which plagues the consciousness of most people. This characteristic is differentiated from the "hearing voices," which denotes some mental illnesses. This internal narration is, for most people, the voice of their desires, judgments, or fears. This internal voice can provide a creative or generous aspect to the personality, and it is usually responsible for frayed tempers, emotional eating, and other negative traits.

(Image courtesy of Allthingsworkplace.com)

Dan Harris discusses his initial skepticism of calming this voice with meditation. He explains that his first impression considered meditation to be the territory of hippies or other alternative personalities who seem to be the personification of soothing pan pipe music. He also considered that since his internal voice was constantly chattering, it would be an impossible task to clear his mind even for just a few moments. There is an acknowledgment that most people have a biased view of meditation.

Many people connect meditation to alternative lifestyles, which hold no appeal to most. However, there has been research, which has shown that meditation can actually modify the pathways of the brain. In order to explore these potential benefits fully, people should ignore the hyped claims of many gurus and simply consider that meditation may be able to increase happiness by 10%, which is a large number in terms of happiness. While this is a rough estimate, it does represent a significant return on investment. The main aim of *10% Happier: How I Tamed the Voice in My Head, Reduced Stress Without Losing My Edge, and Found Self-Help That Actually Works* is to demystify meditation and reassure people that quieting the internal voice will not compromise creativity; it can allow positive changes to occur.

Key Take-Aways

- People are not stuck permanently with the difficult elements of their personality, such as shyness or hot-headedness. These elements are actually learned skills that can be corrected using meditation.
- There is a developing subculture of professional people who are improving their focus, controlling their emotional roller-coaster, and taming their addictions using meditation. This group includes athletes, executives, and even members of the military.

CHAPTER 1

SUMMARY

Here, you will discover the background and history of Dan Harris. He begins by explaining that he experienced a very public low point, which was a panic attack live on air in 2004. Over five million people were watching during his panic attack, and there is a first-hand account of the sensations and symptoms he was feeling during a news desk segment on *Good Morning America*. This account is very moving, as Harris explains how his internal voice was chattering about the pressures of being on live television and how he must "do" something, while he was trying to fight the panic and carry on with his report. Harris acknowledges that this meltdown on air was the result of focusing all his energy on adventure and career advancement while giving no attention to any other aspect of this life.

The opening chapter covers the career path from college graduate to working at a local station, and on through to his work for ABC. Starting as a reporter and anchor at a local station at 22 was an instant challenge for Harris, who found the work fascinating, yet immensely challenging. After seven years of progressing to larger markets, Harris was hired as a co-anchor at ABC. This chapter covers mentoring with experienced anchor Peter Jennings, who was a constructive yet somewhat scary influence on young reporters at the station. The position of news correspondent allowed for travel around the world, pitching new story ideas and claiming as much air time as possible.

While the advice and guidance of Jennings would generally be affected by his mood at any given moment, it did allow Harris to develop his journalistic talents. He was starting to gain a following. However, the cost for this increased attention his inner voice that was harshly self-critical. After spending time as a war correspondent, Harris returned to New York and began chasing the same high using drugs. This was very risky on both a professional and health level, and it was likely the major contributing factor for the on-screen panic attack.

Key Take-Aways

- The inner voice can fuel a person's base demands for immediate pleasure. It is usually the voice that craves food when you are not hungry, the voice that needs a drink at the end of the day, or the voice that wants to simply be lazy and skip work today.

- The inner voice can also provide a voice to drive your ambition or push you forward.

CHAPTER 2

SUMMARY

Chapter two explores the religious correspondent portion of Harris' career. It documents the lack of religious influence during Harris' childhood and how the inner voice leads Harris to make assumptions about the people he meets during his time as a religious correspondent. Initially, the focus of the news pieces was on the conflict between religion and modern society. This foray into religion led to a number of light-hearted reports about Christian reality television, rock festivals, and ordinary activities that were given a religious slant. However, this shallow exploration of the subject was changed when Harris met pastor Ted Haggard. Harris spent time talking to the pastor and his wife and found that they were not as hard line as many other Religious Right figures. Haggard answered many of the religious questions that Harris was too embarrassed to ask others.

These frank conversations provided a revelation for Harris that he had been guilty of judging evangelical congregations and figures using stereotypes and the criticisms of his inner voice. This revelation led Harris to explore religion a little more deeply. However, the death of his mentor, Peter Jennings, created an intense period of change at the network. The competition at the station intensified, as Harris was tapped for a promotion and an anchor position. As a result, the inner voice loop of comparing work, airtime, and standards of colleagues also became more intense. Harris' inner voice went into overdrive, prompting him to complain and criticize when he felt overlooked by producers, or create scenarios in which lack of an assignment could directly lead to career failure.

Harris developed a kinship with Ted Haggard, meeting him for dinner or corresponding for opinions of developments in the religious community. This was shaken when news broke that the pastor had been living a double life and having an extramarital gay affair. Haggard stopped responding to phone calls and emails, despite the news story losing attention due to the devastation from Hurricane Katrina. Harris met his wife at this time, finding the perfect partner for his inner voice-induced moods and spells of self doubt.

Key Take-Aways

- Religion provides some people with a sense of awe about life and the world around them.
- In order to achieve perspective, sometimes you have to stop and consider your place in the universe.

CHAPTER 3

SUMMARY

This chapter explores the initial introduction to meditation. It documents the meeting with Eckhart Tolle, author and advocate of living in the moment. Since Harris has continued to be preoccupied with the potential dangers to succeeding in his career, such as losing his hair or not getting the right assignments, he drifted back towards exploring religion. Eckhart Tolle's book is recommended to Harris, who begins to explore the concept of living in the moment. While this book discusses the inner voice and trying to quiet the negative commentary being voiced internally, Harris found the book rather useless.

Chapter three also details the symptoms and behaviors of the ego and inner voice. This includes failing to be satisfied, comparing oneself to others, and fueling drama. This focus on the demands of the inner voice can lead many people to never appreciate the present moment. A great number of people are constantly looking to achieving success in the future and reminiscing about the past without considering where they actually are in the present.

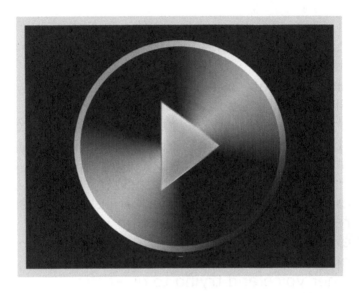

Learn to Live in the NOW with Eckhart Tolle

(Video courtesy of Youtube.com)

Harris identified with this concept of sleepwalking through life. Tolle explains his personal history and inspiration for seeking a path of living in the moment, which resonates with most people. However, while Harris found Tolle inspiring, he felt frustrated by the lack of explanation of how one can be freed from the ego and achieve a worry-free present lifestyle. Harris arranged to interview Tolle as a feature on his show. While Tolle rarely gives interviews, he consented to appear. Tolle was a pleasant character to interview, but Harris found himself struggling to decide if Tolle was genuine or a little mad. While Harris wanted to achieve a more present life without the continual chatter of his inner voice, he was still unsure exactly how this could be accomplished. Harris recognized that living in the moment provides a calm and collected way to deal with life, but he simply could not grasp how this would mesh with dealing with the stress and pressure of his career.

Key Take-Aways

- If you want to make changes, you must be willing to try something new.
- If each moment of your life is never right because you are rushing to the next, you will feel continually stressed.

CHAPTER 4

SUMMARY

This area explores the issues of meditation and living in the moment. Harris meets Deepak Chopra during a *Nightline* debate in which Chopra is facing off against a pastor for the topic of whether Satan exists. Harris was relatively unfamiliar with Chopra's work, but he had the opportunity to meet with him for an interview prior to the debate. He took this opportunity to discuss his own confusion and frustration with the issue of living in the moment. Chopra was not quite as cryptic as Eckhart Tolle, but even he could not provide an insight into how to achieve living in the moment while struggling with the pressures of everyday life.

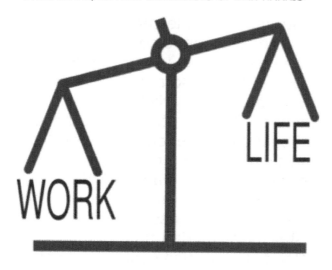

(Image courtesy of Elementarymatters.com)

The chapter documents Harris' struggles to talk about the subject with colleagues, family, and friends. Most people voiced the typical reaction to meditation and this type of enlightenment with gentle mockery and confusion. Harris had the opportunity to meet with Chopra again for a news feature, he found him to be interesting, yet incomprehensible. It was this confusion that led Harris and his team to launch a story series investigating the self-help industry. Self-help is unregulated and generates $11 billion per year.

With many people converting from organized religions to self-help, it had become a hot topic, which was perfect for journalistic exploration. This series of features allowed Harris to visit the two authors of *The Secret*, which had become a national phenomenon. However, Harris found the underlying message (you need to attract what you want) a little disturbing, almost blaming people who are victimized by illness or natural disaster for attracting their own problems. Harris also spoke to people who were so invested in self-help gurus that they didn't have enough money to pay their bills.

Key Take-Aways

- Is the self-help industry about helping or making a profit?
- People need to feel passion, but is passion possible without stress?

CHAPTER 5

SUMMARY

Chapter five details the meeting with the influential guru Dr. Mark Epstein. Harris' girlfriend gave him two of Epstein's books. She had read some of Epstein's work years before and considered that the writings of the psychiatrist and Buddhist may be beneficial to him. After reading the books, Harris realized that many of the principles documented in the work of Tolle was actually derived from Buddhism. The chapter details that people need not believe in the principles of rebirth, enlightenment, and karma to benefit from Buddhist principles.

This includes the information that Buddha never claimed to be a prophet or a god. The legend of Buddha is that he was born in what is now Nepal, 500 years before Jesus Christ. He was the son of a regional king, and he was prophesied to be either a great spiritual leader or a powerful king. When Buddha was young, his father protected him from the world behind the palace walls, but he eventually ran away to explore the world as a wandering monk. After six years, he achieved enlightenment and was reborn as the Buddha.

The philosophy of Buddhism is that nothing lasts forever. All people will die, beauty fades, monarchies fall, and it is all played out within an infinite universe. This doctrine of faith differs greatly from many religions, which promise salvation and encourages followers to achieve an understanding that true happiness can be achieved when you understand "the wisdom of insecurity." However, Harris remained confused by the concept of "letting go" and whether this meant adopting a passive attitude. He arranged a meeting with Epstein, who provided Harris with a list of resource materials and introduced him to a group of Jewish professionals who were attempting to translate Eastern wisdom into Western ideas.

Key Take-Aways

- Eastern spirituality is becoming adopted by many professionals in the Western world. Although not necessarily converting to Buddhism, there are many people who are using the Buddhist principles to develop a calmer, stress-free lifestyle.

- Adopting the present moment philosophy does not restrict the range of emotions. People living in the moment can still experience anger, joy, sadness, and passion.

CHAPTER 6

SUMMARY

Here, Harris explores the power associated with negative thinking, detailing the growing trend of mainstream practitioners, such as therapists, recommending meditation to ease stress and help people cope with the pressures of daily life. There are simple instructions on how to perform basic meditation, and Harris explains that after a 5-minute meditation session while on vacation, he began to work a similar session into his daily routine. There is reassurance that fidgeting thoughts and feeling an itch or discomfort when beginning to meditate is common. However, there is also the assurance that it gets easier over time, allowing you to focus on breathing and the present moment, which is especially important during stagnant moments in your day, such as when you are sitting at a red light.

He also discusses the concept of mindfulness or taking notes of what emotion is affecting the mind before becoming overwhelmed by it. These notes are simply applying a gentle mental label to a feeling or sensation. This can allow people to recognize their emotions without acting on them. For example, if you recognize you are feeling anger, this can allow you to take a moment before losing your temper and shouting at your colleague, spouse, or anyone else "responsible" for your mood.

Mark Epstein expresses the concept as allowing us the potential to "examine our self hatred" without any attempt to alter it, love it, or make it go away. While this is potentially a controversial explanation, it does reassure that meditation will not turn people into mindless, emotionless drones. Tara Brach uses the method of RAIN. This allows you to Recognize, Allow, Investigate and Non-identify any feelings or mental chatter. Each stage facilitates understanding what emotion is on your mind, allows it to be present, and checks if it is affecting you physically, before preventing you from identifying with the emotion and not allowing it to be simply a passing state of mind. While this may not solve the underlying problem, it can prevent people from rushing into negative action blindly.

Key Take-Aways

- Living in the present moment does not mean not feeling emotions. Rather, it provides the opportunity to explore the feeling without acting on impulse.

- Negative thinking may not be eliminated, but by acknowledging your feeling, you can reduce the insistence of your inner voice.

CHAPTER 7

SUMMARY

This section details Harris' experience of a 10-day meditation retreat recommended to him. It provides a day-by-day explanation of how the meditation retreat affected Harris, and what he was feeling at each stage. The retreat was isolated from the outside world, with no talking permitted except during one-on-one mentoring sessions. The days were structured into meditation sessions, both inside the retreat and walking meditation, with vegan Buddhist-inspired cuisine. This would appear to be a radical approach to meditation, and the chapter details how most people struggle with the reality of not talking, refraining from phone calls, avoiding Internet access, and keeping from other modern distractions for 10 days.

(Lotus Position: Photo courtesy of Wikipedia.org)

There is an explanation that the retreat is not the place for sitting and reading, but rather a place to contemplate and meditate at every opportunity. This can create a rollercoaster of emotions, from basic fidgeting irritation to releasing sadness and joy when performing metta meditation. This involves everything from concentrating on sending out good mental vibrations to mental pictures of loved ones, difficult people, acquaintances, and all other beings.

This latter form of meditation is a little closer to the "hippie" image many people think of when they consider meditation. However, this can allow people to explore their emotions further while being in the moment, which can be beneficial for even beginners to meditation.

The difficulties experienced by Harris during his 10 days are enumerated, including the worry that the retreat was not working properly for him. He seeks counsel from the retreat teachers, who explain that meditation isn't about trying too hard; many people experience highs and lows during such as intense retreat. This type of varying emotion and feeling is common during meditation, and the aim is not to simply do it right, but just explore whatever emotion or feeling is present.

Key Take-Aways

- Meditation is not about creating a joyous or elated high, but instead the focus should be on exploring the emotions and feelings in the present moment.

- Meditation retreats provide the opportunity for intense adjustment, but it is possible to explore living in the moment in only a few minutes each day.

CHAPTER 8

SUMMARY

Harris explores the development of the "10% happier" ratio. Harris developed the phrase during discussions with family, friends, and colleagues. Many people are interested in meditation, but there is a stigma that people who meditate are part of a cult or walking automatons. After returning from the 10-day retreat, Harris discovered that his friends and family were interested in where he had been and what it was like. However, there was still embarrassment when people were questioning why a meditation retreat would be of benefit. When a colleague asked Harris about "the whole meditation thing," he merely replied that it made him 10% happier. This is a realistic figure, which is a far cry from the gurus and self-help experts who claim that their program or method will change lives completely.

That phrase, 10% happier, became the immediate response to any meditation questions, and it allowed

Harris to explain why he was interested in exploring meditation further. While many experts intimate that meditation allows people to feel 100% happier, for most people, 10% represents a great return on their investment and effort. Harris does not claim that meditation is a cure for all issues, but that it allows people to become more resilient against negative inner voice chatter and the stresses of modern life. This allows people to develop insight into their own world. Rather than dwell on the thoughts of losing a job or not receiving a promotion, people can explore the positive aspects of their lives, such as if the worst happened and a person lost employment, he or she would still have a partner, family, friends, and lots of love. It is a way for people to stay out of their own way.

Key Take-Aways

- Meditation allows you to quiet the inner voice and achieve insight into your actual situation. This is a positive experience, allowing you to examine your current situation to make positive changes.
- Meditation allows a glimpse into the mind, and it provides the opportunity for a close look at the fundamentals of life.

CHAPTER 9

SUMMARY

This section explores the far-reaching impact of meditation. While most of the Buddhist philosophy has not become mainstream, the practice of meditation is being explored by the military and professionals from a variety of industries. Meditation has been described as the "new caffeine" with a number of medical and psychological benefits, including correcting irritable bowel syndrome, relieving depression and addiction, and decreasing stress, binge eating, smoking, and loneliness.

A number of studies have concluded that meditation reduces the level of stress hormones and provides a boost to the immune system. While many of these benefits have been ascribed to meditation for decades, research out of Harvard University actually used MRI scans to determine that meditation increased the gray matter of the areas of the brain linked to compassion and self-awareness. The scans also showed a decrease in the regions of the brain linked to stress. This provided hard data for skeptics, showing that meditation increased the areas of the brain that regulate base urges and primal feelings.

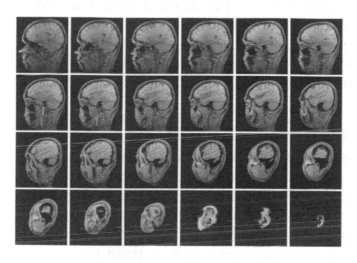

(MRI: Photo courtesy of Commons.wikimedia.org)

This research is still in its infancy, yet it has highlighted the hypothesis that the brain changes as a response to experiences. This contradicts the old belief that the brain was only developing during childhood and adolescence, ceasing to change once adulthood was reached. This highlights the possibility to shape the brain using mediation, similar to the way you build the muscles of the body using proper diet and regular exercise.

Even Big Business appears to have taken note of the potential offered by meditation. Large corporations are now providing meditation rooms for employees to become better, more focused leaders, with greater creativity and innovation.

This approach contradicts the popular working edicts of multitasking and always being busy. However, many market leaders are now embracing the approach of taking a short mindfulness break to improve work focus and productivity, concentrating on completing one task properly, rather than rushing through several at once.

This new corporate trend has been discussed in the *Harvard Business Review* and the *Wall Street Journal*, and it is being taught in business schools as a valid strategy for productivity and success.

The marines explored the possibility of using meditation to cope with Post Traumatic Stress Disorder, to ensure that troops are less reactive and vulnerable to the provocation tactics of insurgents.

Key Take-Aways

- Meditation is no longer considered an unusual practice. Many mainstream organizations have recognized the potential offered by meditation. They have embraced it as a method of increasing productivity and creativity.

- While meditation has become more popular, it is ironic that this Buddhist-inspired practice is being used by capitalists and those engaged in violent activities. Without compassion, meditation cannot reach its full potential.

CHAPTER 10

SUMMARY

Harris has the opportunity to meet the Dalai Lama. While most people view the Dalai Lama as a revered Buddhist figure, he can also be a symbol of the elements of Buddhism that many people struggle to embrace. The interview with the Dalai Lama is interesting, as it explores his support for the scientific research being conducted into meditation. The Dalai Lama believes that this research will not contradict his beliefs, and if new information is discovered, it will allow his beliefs to be modified. The Dalai Lama appears to be a very pleasant and gregarious individual who admits that he occasionally loses his temper and experiences negative emotions. He has played a pivotal role in the research conducted by the scientific community into meditation, providing funding and inspiration.

The chapter also explores the Dalai Lama's concept of "self cherishing." This is said to be a natural concept by which developing concern for other people's well being can actually be of benefit. This aspect of being "wise selfish" has been explored in research conducted at the Emory University campus. The research team provided participants with a course of compassion meditation before exposing them to stressful situations. The team found that those who completed the compassion meditation had significantly lower levels of the stress hormone cortisol. This suggests that by having compassion for others, the body copes with stress better. This has been confirmed with brain scans showing an act of kindness registering in a similar way to eating chocolate.

Research conducted by the University of Wisconsin Madison found that there was increased activity in the areas of the brain linked to understanding and empathy after compassion meditation.

This aspect is more closely related to the original Buddhist teachings. Buddha taught his followers morality and generosity before instructing in meditation. This could be because concentration would be easier to attain if you were not inner voice chatting about being mean or bad to others. This is documented in the list of benefits for meditation compiled by the Buddha, which includes sleeping better, appearing more radiant, and being reborn into a happier realm.

This type of meditation can be very beneficial, since, although you may still feel irritated, you will no longer have the delusion that people are irritating you on purpose, and you can stop before taking negative action.

Key Take-Aways

- Acts of kindness and compassion help people cope with stress. This reduction in the stress hormone cortisol could have long term health benefits, including a reduced risk of heart disease and certain forms of cancer.

- Is it possible to be compassionate and driven in your career? Harris struggled with the balance of compassion while participating in the high stakes world of competitive journalism.

CHAPTER 11

SUMMARY

Harris explores the balance between compassionate living in the moment and prospering in the modern workplace. He chronicles another major change in staffing at ABC and the impact it had on the dynamics of the network. Harris adopted the approach of not trying to impress the new head of ABC and simply remaining Zen about the situation. However, he found that he was not being chosen for high profile stories. Instead of flaring up and complaining as he had in the past, Harris chose to ponder the situation, not wanting to be uncompassionate towards his colleagues. This situation is what many professional people fear about becoming Zen.

Harris became unassertive and took a passive approach to being overlooked. However, the situation became worse, so he scheduled a meeting with the network head. This meeting was very illuminating; it provided the confirmation that Harris was simply not working as hard to be noticed. He had developed a passive attitude both on and off screen, which was being detrimental to his career. Harris was advised by Mark Epstein to simply "hide the Zen" while at work. Some degree of aggression in the workplace is often necessary, and acting Zen can make people appear passive, uninterested, or weak.

This adopting of a meek attitude is a common mistake when interpreting the dharma of Buddhism. This meekness and detachment can be very counterproductive, even nihilistic. However, it is possible to balance the dogma. While it is good to live in the moment and adopt a transcendent view of the world, you should also retain common sense. This can be achieved with the adoption of a non attachment mindset. This simply means do your very best, but realize that some things are simply out of your control. You can strive to succeed, but it should be tempered with the concept that the final outcome may very well be outside of your influence.

This chapter details the 10 rules of the "way of the worrier," which include "don't be a jerk," "hide the Zen," "meditate," and "humility prevents humiliation." These rules for the "corporate samurai" are self-explanatory, yet they combine to allow people to balance a calm attitude with the attributes needed to succeed in the modern competitive workplace.

Key Take-Aways

- Balance is essential to succeed in the modern world. While many may wish to be completely Zen, this may be detrimental. A balance between total nihilism and competitive jerk is the best way to achieve Zen in the workplace.

- Discard the concept of a Zen attitude equating to being meek. This is a common mistake, and it can compromise your happiness.

EPILOGUE

SUMMARY

The epilogue covers the development of enlightenment, which is a gradual process for most people. Achieving enlightenment is not likely to happen the first time you begin to meditate, but according to Dr. Judson Brewer, when the brain has experienced significant amounts of mindfulness, it can "eventually create a self reinforcing spiral." This could lead to the brain retreating from negative emotions, such as hatred or greed, which would be enlightenment. Others argue that since you can train the body to be faster or stronger, it is also possible to practice being compassionate and wise to achieve enlightenment.

The book concludes with an update on Harris' career progression together with how his journey has changed his way of thinking. He reports that a number of his friends and family have begun to explore meditation for themselves. While Harris makes no claim that the book has changed his life completely, he does reveal that he is at least 10% happier.

He feels calmer and in control of his life, without the constant worry and commentary of his inner voice.

PUTTING IT TOGETHER

Dan Harris' *10% Happier* is a great chronicle of the exploration of meditation and adopting a present moment approach to life. Unlike many "guru" style books, this book provides a real world insight into meditation without wild claims for instant change. The reader can follow Harris' path of exploration and learning, which is told in a humorous and self deprecating tone.

Many people are curious about meditation, and *10% Happier* provides great insight into how meditation can be of benefit. Most self-help books are vague about the details of how to accomplish your goals, but *10% Happier* includes step-by-step instructions for basic meditation techniques. He discusses the terminology in layman's terms, explaining the abstract concepts often used and quoted by gurus and experts. This can be a great help to those who are relatively new to the concepts of Buddhism and meditation. The book details how Harris went about his research into the benefits of meditation. Readers will find many things to take from the pages.

The book does not claim to provide all the answers to life's issues, nor does it provide insight into how to quiet one's inner voice, rather it provides a unique insight into how a person can become 10% happier and learn to use his or her inner voice as a productive tool. While this may not please every reader, it is a down-to-earth guide to the benefits of adopting a new approach and using meditation in everyday life.

With the growing pressures of the modern workplace, this book provides a great opportunity to explore a new way to manage stress and reduce self-doubt. Harris' true story highlights the possibility of reducing stress without compromising ambition or the competitive edge needed in most industries. While it may not answer every question one might have about the potential benefits of meditation, it provides a great resource for beginners.

ABOUT THE BOOK'S AUTHOR

Dan Harris is one of the co-anchors of *Nightline* and ABC's weekend edition of *Good Morning America*. He has reported from areas all around the world, covering conflicts in Iraq, Afghanistan, and Palestine. He has produced numerous investigative pieces in America, Cambodia, the Congo, and Haiti. Despite being agnostic, he also spent a great number of years covering the faith scene of America, especially evangelicals.

Harris grew up with a younger brother in the Boston area with both parents practicing medicine. He was attracted to journalism from a young age, and it became his career focus after leaving college. He began working at local news stations, making career progressions to larger stations in the Boston and Maine areas before starting work at ABC. He has worked at ABC for over 14 years and credits many of his colleagues at the network for providing the inspiration to become a better journalist.

Harris has made many friends in his journey to discover meditation, and he credits his Jewbu friends with changing his mind about the possibilities and benefits offered by meditation. He is now successfully "hiding the Zen" while working, and he has inspired a number of colleagues, family members, and friends to try meditation for themselves.

Harris is now married to his then girlfriend Bianca, and they live in New York City. He has received a number of awards for his journalistic contributions, including an Emmy in 2009 for his *Nightline* report on "How to buy a child in ten hours," and an Edward R. Murrow Award for his report on a young Iraqi man who received help to move to America. Harris graduated from Colby College in Waterville Maine. He also holds an honorary doctorate degree from Colby and the Massachusetts College of Liberal Arts. Harris continues to make time in his schedule to meditate every day.

Readers Who Enjoyed This Ebook Might Also Enjoy...

Dan Harris' _10% Happier_ (the full book)

Dr. Terry Wahl's _The Wahls Protocol_

Jane Olson's _Counting Calories_

Save Time Summaries' _Grain Brain: The Surprising Truth about Wheat, Carbs, and Sugar (Your Brain's Silent Killers) by David Perlmutter -- Summary, Review & Analysis_

#

CPSIA information can be obtained at www.ICGtesting.com
Printed in the USA
LVOW01s2258230514

387191LV00013B/375/P